A Bit of Our World

Sarah Sun

Dixie W Publishing Corporation U.S.A.

Published by
Dixie W Publishing Corporation
Montgomery, Alabama, U.S.A.
http://www.dixiewpublishing.com

Printed in the United States of America
9 8 7 6 5 4 3 2 1
First Printing: January 2021

Library of Congress Control Number: 2021930190
ISBN-13: 978-1-68372-317-2

Sarah Sun is currently a student with a passionate joy in writing. Through poetry she wishes to show to the world what is felt in the heart and thoughts every day that can only be expressed through words. She currently lives in New York, US.

To Cynthia, the mother bird

who taught me to fly.

Table of Contents

PART 1
NATURE

When It Rains…

When it rains
Sometimes I would spend hours listening to the pitter-
patter
And drip, drip, drip of the drops
That are like tears
Falling from a stormy gray sky

They drizzle upon the ground
Collecting to form puddles
Swirling and swirling around
In delicate patterns

Sliding down the silver-paned windows,
So everything outside,

Reality, is blurred

Like when we are trapped

In desolate times

Every day details are blurred

Cars passing on the streets

Water sloshing as the wheels

Leave tracks in the mud

Headlights an unearthly glow

In the hazy downpour

Like red moons

Against the stormy night

And as the many cars drive

The moons all blur together

In strings and strings of stars

Bright upon an inky canvas

Remember, though, that just like the rain

Gliding down the window

The blurred feelings

Will be cleared

And the next day, when the sun rises

From the gray mountains in the distance

The rainwater is gone

Swept back up to their haven in the sky

Just like our sadness

Building and building up until

We can't hold the sorrow in anymore

And they wet our cheeks

And drop, like rain, into our laps

Soon there are no more tears

And after some time, the sadness will be let out again

Just remember, every time you cry

The sun will dry up your tears

Just like it does

To the rain

I guess it's true when they say

Rain is the Earth crying

Tears pouring down

Because it can't be held in anymore

Our sorrows coursing inside of us

Searching for an outlet

A place to drip

To a realm far away

Staining Earth's cheeks

The wet soil

Overflowing rivers

Rising oceans

And the water, flowing

Everywhere

But soon the rain dries

Sun shines through

The many colors of a rainbow

Drying the water

Earth's eyes are again dry

And a smile

Spreads slowly

Across our faces

Memory of Nature

Where have all the flowers gone?

Their delicate selves have withdrawn

They've curled up, like they are scared

Black petals of dark and despair

Where have all the waters gone?

They no longer shine at dawn

The river and the streams run dry

No tears to spill from weary eyes

Where have all animals gone?

The subtle birds and the baby faun

The chitter and chatter leave only an trace

Of the wonders that have been erased

Where has all the sunlight gone?

It used to wake at morn and yawn

A memory of warmth upon my skin

A ghost of what things once have been

Then Where Will You Go?

I know you travel the windblown lands
And dance across the sun kissed sands
But when the day fades with the sun in tow
Then where will you go?

I know you laugh under moonlight's beams
And splash in glancing waterfall's streams
But when the river's currents cease to flow
Then where will you go?

I know you soar with the birds and breeze
Watch the world from sycamore trees
But when the singing winds don't blow

Then where will you go?

I know you run from who you are

From every wound, and every scar

But when your tired legs begin to slow

Then where will you go?

The Moonlight Dance

Jewels embedded in starry night
The blackness devours the beads of light
An ocean of depthless inky darkness
A lurking place of fear and plight

But to night-time's fear we are immune
We see beauty, in the stars and moon
They sing in notes of moonlit silver
The evening, playing a cheerful tune

So join this night in its swing and sway
To bid farewell and welcome to the rising day
We'll frolic to a place beyond our minds

To a place that exists far away

Here to waltz, twirl and entrance

To swirl and jump and turn and prance

For the sky's beckoning to you tonight

To come join it in the moonlight dance

Stars and Flowers

A million stars late night time reveals
Dotting the sky like flowers in a field
They sparkle and whisper tales of the past
Of the empires and traditions they outlast
A million smiles that guide our way
But fade and relinquish to the coming day

A million flowers spread wide like the sky
Like the million of stars that they defy
A short lifetime, waiting when
They flourish the next year and grow again
They guide us through our lives thereof
Together with the stars above

Moon and Sea

The air is sweet, out by the sea
In the sky, the moon beams at me
Water laps quietly, out by the sea
A warm smile, the moon beams at me

Wafting salty breeze, sleep under night
Walk below moon's solemnly light
Soft, playful waves, sleep under night
Gaze up at moon's solemnly light

Dawn long off, waiting to be found
Silvery moonlight, upon the ground
Dozing sun, waiting to be found

Shifting golden sand upon the ground

Foam sizzles along the ocean floor
Sparkles glimmer across the shore
Fish burrow into the ocean floor
Seashells embedded across the shore

Along the ocean walks you and I
Under a brightly speckled sky
Into the sea swims you and I
Tread water under a painted sky

The air is sweet, out by the sea
In the sky, the moon beams at me
Water laps quietly, out by the sea
A warm smile, the moon beams at me

Above the Clouds

the clouds break across the horizon,

golden sunshine filtering through,

shafts of light fall like rain,

shimmering in the air

like the aurora borealis of the day.

before dawn,

silver moonlight glows in a halo of gray clouds;

smoldering fire sets flame

among wisps of smoke and fog,

pale shadows flickering

between the billowing haze.

a wall of vapor

piles between me and the universe out there;

some days the wall is heavy,

brick by brick squeezed together,

and other times barely a whisper

on a sunny day.

gazing from below at the impenetrable fortress

that separates me from the sun,

i'm not trapped,

but rather imagining the world

where the light is never blocked.

it's on the days when the clouds are heavy

that i feel feather light;

if i could somehow fly above the wall,

above the rain soon to come,

i could walk above the clouds.

Heart of White

Along foaming beach
Walks you and I
Under a moonlit
Star-filled sky

Atop silver water
Swims graceful birds
Beauty and light
Too much for words

Teardrop water sprays
From flapping wings
Two glistening swans

Best all beautiful things

Both graceful swans

Long necks drink

Sip starlight water

Of green-felt spring

Along foaming beach

They form a heart

A smile, for love

That won’t break apart

Tendrils and Waves

Seeking tendrils reach out their fluid arms, rising from places dark as the eternal abyss, smooth as the night sky

Foaming bubbles, white as the moonlight glancing off the surface of the dark sea, greeted them with muted cries

The waters lap greedily at the beach, grasping onto the sands, and pulling them into the dark, where they are swept away

They travel out, those small grains of sand, following the ocean's currents, to find a new home on lonely shore, I pray

The waves skim the surface of the water, little spirals atop a land of inky blackness, tossing and turning

They splash, leaving imprints and ripples on a bumpy surface, always moving, always churning

The sands are still floating, lost, lost, lost… ashes floating and dying in the wake of a fire burning

Palm trees flail their long leaves, dancing a strange duet with the wind, reaching, grasping, curling around empty air

We humans skip upon the beach, the breeze blowing to and fro curling tendrils of our sun-kissed hair

The sands drift gently across the ocean, searching, seeking, until they land on another shore, join the family at the other end

And there they sit, under the sun, waiting for the tendrils and waves to grasp and bring them on the same, long journey again

The Sea

The sea is stretches of vacant land
Followed by masses of barren sand
    The inside dark
        The surface bland
A teeming demon of claws and fangs

The sea is a base of shining life
Color and type and shape alike
    The families large
        The members rife
The many creatures bathe in delight

The sea is a place of certain death

A place of perilous watery depths

Can’t open my eyes

Can’t take a breath

A realm of danger and risk and threat

The sea is a domain of many wonders

A haven from the storms and thunder

A beauteous mystery

A magical under

A serene world a blanket of blue covers

Ripples on Water

Upon the surface, the ripple sways

Under the sky's smiling gaze

    The winds dance

        The ocean plays

The sun sets the water ablaze

The ripples trace a circular trail

They shimmer and swirl in the storming gale

    The ocean screams

        The drafts wail

A raging contest in the air I inhale

The ripples draw a line of light

As they writhe and wriggle in delight

A starry sky

A silent night

While they douse and quench and ignite

The ripples lay under moonlight's beams

Flowing silently in river streams

I gaze alight

At their kindly beams

They sleep calm under peaceful dreams

A Raven's Call

A whoosh of whispering air

A flicker of a wing

Black and smooth as the night sky

For whom does this dark bird sing?

It soars, flies, dances

Swift as the breeze

Sharp as the edge of the knife

Shrewd as the deadly seas

Those glittering eyes

Dark, endless holes

Like a unknown gateway

To a million souls

Into the air it flies
It's form invisible against the night
Its voice a siren's song
That leads many to fake light

Their chatter is not a secret
They are made to enthrall
But, animals out there, you better hope
You don't hear the raven's call

Run With Me

Parting clouds give way to raining sunlight,
golden drops drifting like feathers from azure skies,
shafts of water light as air falling
from the heavens up high

I see you,
golden fur gleaming in matching sunlight,
paws lightly bouncing
over the flower-ridden meadow,
tongue sipping from
the elixir slipping from the sky

I beckon,
and we go flying across the flowers,

rainbows like paint dotted across a canvas,
laughing and splashing in the sun's water,
the fantasy world magic we can see

We reach the end of the meadow,
and turn back around
to the blossoms and gemstones,
because the flowers are the rainbows
and the sunlight is the treasure at the end

You and I smile,
your tongue flopping in joy,
and looking towards the diamonds
that glistened in the grass, I turn towards you, and say-
run with me

Breath of a Pond

Gurgle, gurgle

The pond surface is still, lily pads drifting across a surface so blue, it is like the sky fell into the water, the clouds drifting across in shimmers of light from the midday sun

Leaves hang over the clear waters, dew bunching up in strings of pearls, slowly dripping onto the water lilies that sit silently under them: one two one, one two one

Click, click

Soft ripples stir the pond's surface as a dragonfly gently lands on the lily, shaking out its wings heavy with dew, perching on the edge, waiting to again take flight

Translucent wings flutter gently, water again dripping onto the water lily, the sun's blaze reflecting off the surface of the water, bending it into strange patterns of light

Croak, croak

The frogs perch on lily pads, singing their throaty morning song, webbed feet extended and necks arched in the laziness of the time when the sun is high

Underneath the grown ones, small tadpoles dart here and about, playing their games beneath the still waters, flickering and dancing by

Splash, splash

Snapping turtles drift on the waters, floating about, their flippers pedaling slowly through the gentle currents, shells a haven for small animals to perch on

They crawl slowly onto the grass, stretching out to warm themselves in the bright sun, and there they will stay until the day's light is gone

Shriek, shriek

Predators swoop above the treetops, calling and screeching to one another, curved beaks seeking, sharp eyes searching

Their wings flap in mighty bursts, the birds of prey circling, watching with carefully scrutiny the currents beneath the surface, steadily churning

Chirp, chirp

The small, flying birds swoop in small spirals, calling out cheerfully to each other in incandescent birdsong

The hummingbirds and robins trill in swirling notes, like the nightingales singing in soprano among the forest, where nature's music belongs

Swish, swish

The fish swim around, seeking shade under the wide, green lily pads, small bubbles bursting from their puckered lips

Some swim alone, while others stick together in giant schools, swishing their tails in their underwater bliss

Quack, quack

The ducks swim blissfully, webbed feet angling out of their snow white feathers and paddling gently in the water, gliding

They duck into the bushes upon the shore, behind the thick leaves of marine plants, cheerfully living and hiding

Buzz, buzz

Bees buzz around in looping, carefree spirals, as if

drawing dotted lines upon the bright blue paper of the sky

They soar up into the clouds, where the birds dwell, above the pond, where the fish glide, and into the trees, where the bluebirds fly

PART 2
LIFE & FEELINGS

Stars Can't Shine Without the Dark

I used to think in our perfect world, there was bad and there was good

If you told me otherwise, in the past, I doubt I would've understood

However, we all change, do we not? We fight our own bloody war

But we cringe from the battle, not from fear, but because we don't want to see any more

There's no distinction between good and bad like there is white and black

The understanding of the shades of gray is something our childhood lacks

For we're all mixed, light and dark, with no clear line

in between

We all tell lies, but within is truth, because we know what lies unseen

It's opposite of just a solid line that separates heaven from hell

Fairytales show perfect pictures, but they're just stories that we tell

For everyone has a side that's dark, a side that some don't see

But, deep inside, we strive to be the best that we could be

For a flower, beauty from the earth, can't bloom without the rain

And our shield can't fully form if it's not tested against the pain

You can't build a fire if you don't know how to make a spark

For its eternal, and we all know, stars can't shine without the dark

Memories and Loss

Sometimes we wonder who we are
Joy and hope, or wounds and scars
What will we leave behind when we fall?
Or if there will be nothing left at all

We think, what is our purpose in living?
Laughing and crying, taking and giving
We dig through life for something to save
But mislead the hurried road we pave

Perhaps our words will be lost to time
But leaves the traces that are sublime
And though pain will always find your way

There's always a new start the next day

So now we know what marks us best

What's left behind more than the rest

It's is thin web of peace that spans across

The milestones and memories, tragedy and loss

Drops of My Heart

a million buttons, heavy and full
with all the tears our eyes will spill
a cliff below, and the sky above
i held the rope, life forgot to pull

one, two, three buttons, four
sew one button on, and then one more
each one a feeling, each one a heart
to sell away at the store

two, three, four buttons, five
each one a problem I have survived
sew and sell my fear and regrets

this is how I stay alive

three, four, five buttons, six
selfish of me, I must admit
pile my burdens onto someone else
whoever wears them, I'm sorry for this

one, two, three drops, four
write one word, then one more
each one a feeling, each one a heart
drops of ink upon the floor

black tears spill from weary pen
cry in letters again and again
write with tired hands until
the words reach the story's end

my heart's map that i've drawn

a sun to rise with the dawn

like the stars when ink fills the sky

the words are there when i am gone

Laughing Through Tears

The things unique to humankind
Are the emotions we can feel
The hate, pain, love and joy
That makes our lives more real

It's the memories and the laughter
That we are thankful we had
Or the thought that there are good days
Mixed in with the bad

We have our own separate roads
But at some points they'll intersect
We're drops of dew on a spider web

And through those strings we connect

We know there's always hope out there
It's waiting to be found
And there'll be someone to catch you
Before you hit the ground

So life is not just joy and pain
Or learning our strengths and fears
It's finding a star on the darkest nights
And laughing through our tears

Box of My Wishes

box of hope, please come here
to where my bravery touches fear
fight them away, fight them now
till they're something i can bear

box of love, come to me
to my ship atop a lonely sea
i know i'm foolish, or naive, perhaps
but joy is near, possibly

box of joy, let yourself show
come with me wherever i go
battle for me all my scars

vanquish for me all my foes

box of loss, go away now

too much happiness i have to vow

you have no place in my heart

no place for you i will allow

Let My Heart Run Free

my heart used to be trapped
a cage for my emotions
i figured building walls
meant I was strong
but then my human part
was gone

my spirit and feelings
they were cooped up inside
by not letting anyone in
no one could make me cry
was it really enough?
to be so unfeeling and tough

but life didn't listen

my emotions can still be touched

because sometimes, instead of brick

it's better to bend and mold

like elastic

stretching to fit the world

it's the emotions that make us strong

the love that makes us real

for, every heart, both me and you

has the ability to feel

and so, when the walls came crumbling down

to reveal what you can't see

my heart stretched, open once more

i let it run free

Colors of Feeling

Red pencil, pulled roughly across parchment, tip rubbing off in angry streaks, as words strongly felt form

Green pencil, light scattering of life doodled in sketchbooks, in swift, fast strokes

Yellow pencil, bright sunshine pouring onto the paper like rain to the ground, broad colors creating light

Black pencil, scrawling words of sorrow, dark marks like tears pouring off a blank white page

Pencils of all colors, a rainbow of feelings, the life of each different because we control them

The tip will become a stub over time, but sharpen it and it'll become new once more

Like every time we fall to our knees, we'll sharpen our shields and stand back up again

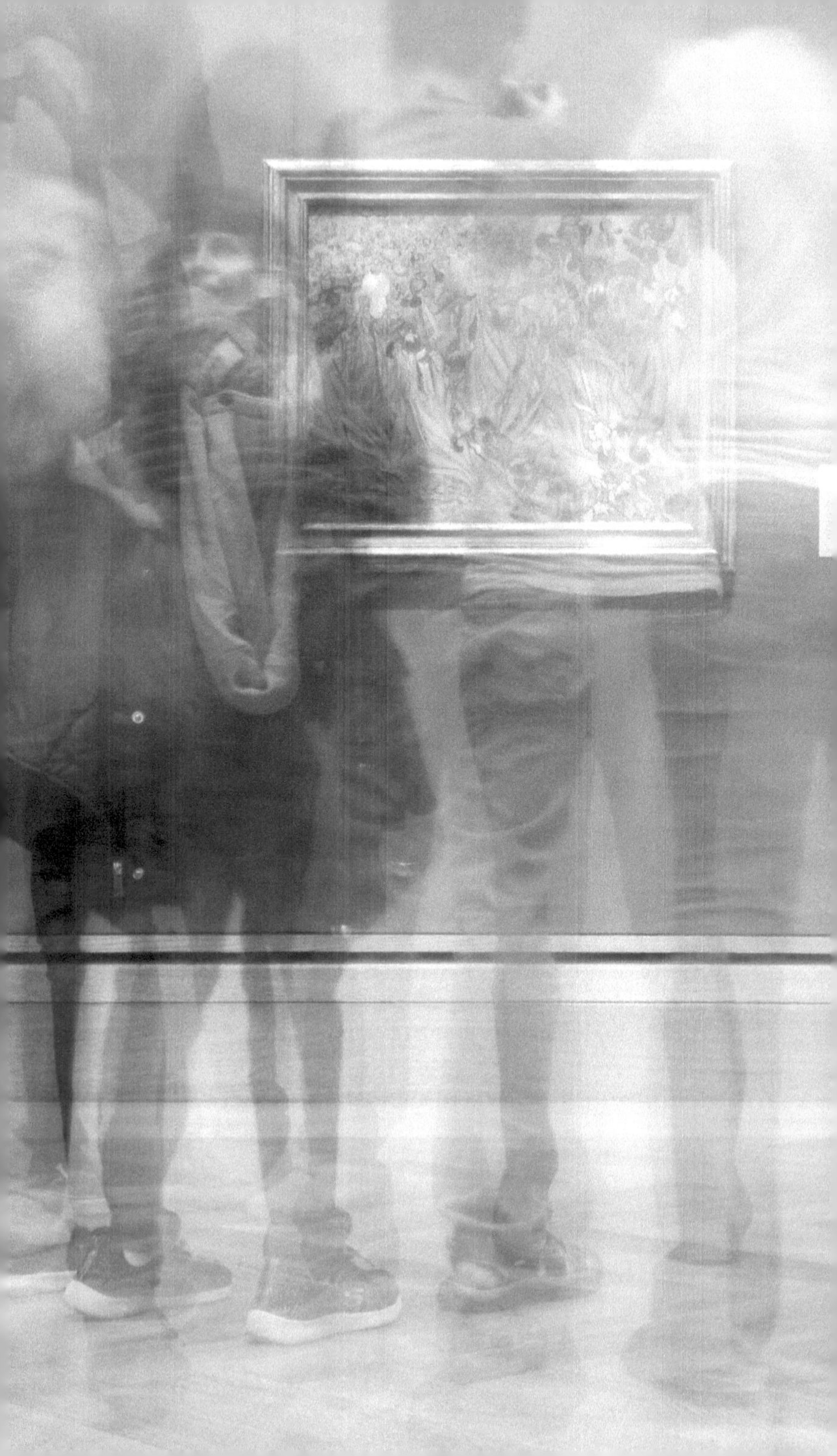

Hidden Portraits

a portrait of a girl,
bright smile on her face
white teeth, red lips,
eyes up in hidden grace

she looks content and well,
not a trouble, not care
like she could hang the moon
and braid stardust through her hair

those eyes, twinkling blue
like the crystals of the sky
say, would a frown crease those corners

should a cloud be passing by?

but, perhaps that smile
hides the troubled frown
camera catches her looking up once
in all the times that she's looked down

because we never will know
what really happened to you
looking at the photo, we can only hope
that the smile was true

---

a portrait of a boy,
mouth turned down in fear
creases of his cheeks collect
every dropping tear

he looks like the world has grown
too heavy for him to bear
he sits in his paper-thin world
waiting for it to tear

the tears pool in his lap
like the water in the sea
you must feel the urge to scream
"why, just leave him be"

but maybe, behind that frown
lies a hidden smile
the acting is so potent, because
he hasn't cried in a while

so no, the photograph is not
a portrait of their soul
because you will never truly know
what made the image whole

Sideways Steps

sometimes I feel

in life,

we walk like

a crab.

always going sideways

not watching

where we're going

hitting problems.

keeping your eyes

forwards, sometimes

is painful, and

no one

likes to meet

their problems

head on.

but sometimes

head on

is the only way

that works,

indeed.

Peace at Last

I'm looking up, up high
Wishing I'm up there in the sky
To take off the burdens of the past
Peace at last, peace at last

I set out upon this quest
To the world of the blessed
Up in the air I am cast
Peace at last, peace at last

In the heavens to which I fly
I look at the ground, but now from the sky

The Crown On My Head

Perhaps, as you stare me down,
you will think your quest complete
For after the war you think you've won
I'm kneeling at your feet
You scorn, a smile on your lips
as you play with my fears
But wait, patience, my friend,
I'll turn the taunting into cheers
Sprawling lazily on your throne,
you deal out your commands
I'll laugh, when you finally find
you have a rebellion on your hands
You'll display your finery, your gilded crown,

lavishly for all to see

The jewels and riches will weigh you down

more than set you free

You're determined to erode your enemies

till no more remains

I can see your surprise when I'm

free from your falling chains

Enough is enough to draw the line

when I won't take any more

I'm much stronger than the person

that sat in tears before

I wonder how proud you will feel

when I'm on the throne instead

I can imagine the disbelief

when the crown's placed on my head

What Lies on the Other Side

An ancient photograph, so old and frail
Of a memory trapped in time
I wonder, does it show his joyful life
Or if the smile is fake sublime

I finger along its time worn edges
The sides patched and frayed
Wondering, was he always smiling like that?
Or if that smile never stayed

I wonder which trail he decided to take
Which crossroads that he chose
But perhaps no one will ever know

When the story here has froze

A single moment, of a whole journey
A flash in one long life
We could never find out his cheerful times
Or his days of worry and strife

I look, I stare, what is that there?
What is that behind the scenes?
I lean forward, and abruptly I fall
As time swirls and convenes

I look around, where have I gone?
It seemed that the worlds crack
I look behind, from where I fell
And there he is, staring back

My mouth agape, my eyes wide
I wonder what has occurred

But finally, it hits me hard
That something absurd has stirred

Wasn't this what I wished for before?
What I've always wanted to see
When I thought a few seconds ago
What his life might be

The world flashes as I travel through
The life he left behind
And I see the laughs and the cries
The hate and joy combined

So life is complex, isn't that true?
A picture not enough to show
The wonders of life that had been lived
The secrets that none know

And remember, before you judge or define

There’s much more that they can hide

For a photograph can’t really catch

What lies on the other side

Your Time Is Up

Tick, tick

One two three

A million seconds

I don't see

Tick, tick

Three two one

Life of ignorance

Is never done

Tick, tick

Four five six

A thousand lessons

Don't seem to stick

Tick, tick

Six five four

The clock will tick

Forever more

Tick, tick

Seven eight nine

Another 10 years

And I'll be fine

Tick, tick

Nine eight seven

What will I

Find in heaven

Tick, tick

Ten eleven twelve

Place this fantasy

Back on the shelf

Tick, tick

Twelve eleven ten

No more time

Our story ends

QUARTZ

The Clock is Ticking

one, two, three

the clock ticking
never-ending
those handles turning
around and around
never stopping

one, two, three

moving along
and us with it
dragging us upon

the path of life
our days are timed

so we strive
to fill that time with all
the joy and memories
of laughter
to make our lives
happy ones

because remember
the clock
is always ticking

one, two, three

BE

FEARLESS

BE

YOU

We Rule Ourselves

It may seem like instructions

Come from all sides

Like the pull of the moon

Controls the ocean tides

As if everyone is there

Just to order you around

Though they don't care to catch you

When your about to hit the ground

Remember that our life

Is thoroughly our own

No one else can choose to sit
Atop our kindly throne

Should we look from above
There's more that we could see

Let your feelings be your own
For that's the best way to be

Unexpected Turns

There are times I forget where to go
Which path I'm supposed to take
It's during those times that I don't know
Success is born from mistake

When our maze is filled with twists and bends
Covered with our aimless prints
But we find when our will amends
That it's only a labyrinth

When mountains stand tall in our way
And on this journey we stand alone
But they'll still be sunshine the next day

When you soar on wings you've grown

When there are crossroads in your trail
And you don't know which to choose
Recall when you run on and on to no avail
That failure comes in different hues

So life's not just about success
Or listing our future's concerns
It's smiling more, worrying less
And besting the unexpected turns

.

Hope

A sparkling mirror, waiting there
The surface bright and clear
I just meandered through daily life
And suddenly, it was here

I don't know what it's trying to show me
What it expects me to do
So I stare thoughtfully at the glass
And then leap and jump right through

I ended up in eternal darkness
A vault of sorrow and pain
Looking back for a way out

And the mirror did not remain

I back off, this eternal night
How it scares me so
Endless black, a gaping hole
And there's no place to go

But what is that there? A single star
Oh, it shines so bright
What is it? It is a single soul
That has begun to fight

The darkness suddenly
Doesn't seem so small
Because that light is for me
It is for us all

Hasn't given in to their fears
That soul glows near and far

It is then that I realize

We can all be a star

So awaken, and you will find embers

When they're hot enough they'll spark

So don't stay trapped, don't stay hidden,

And find the hope in the dark

Happiness

Let us feel joy, waiting when
It slowly finds its way
To us, and all, in this world
So we feel it every day

Merriment, is the rising sun
That battles away the night
For doing what we love with glee
Is doing ourselves right

Battle our way to triumph
Earn our medal of gold
For the story of our happiness
Is a tale that we've all told

Brighten the heart of you and I

Illuminate the hearts of we

For being happy every single day

Is how we all deserve to be

Pixie Dust and Sparkles

i close my eyes,

and the colors burst in my mind,

glitter showering down in all colors

a land of those with wings,

translucent and aglow

with the light of the mystical

a realm of fairies,

pointed toes and small fingers

wrapped around branches of trees

wide eyes bright with the starlight

and fireflies that

drift through the air

shadows dance under the trees

in the wake of the silver rain

of the moon

i open my eyes,

ceiling above welcoming me back

to the land of reality

Wish

Floating Away

I wish I could touch the sky
Be up there, flying up high
To be like a cloud someday
Floating away, away

I wish I could get rid of the lies
Live free like a butterfly
To be a bird, living astray
Floating away, away

I wish I could erase the past
To come hug the peace at last
To somehow find bliss today

Floating away, away

I wish heaven would open the door
Forget the memories from before
The paradise to which I stray
Floating away, away

I wish we live a world of joy
Banish the darkness that we destroy
Come what may, come what may,
For we're floating away, away

Dear Reader, I Wish I Could Tell You This Ends Well

Dear reader, I wish I could tell you this ends well

But no, of this writing our pride has fell

I started this journey with things to say

But all my words are now fading away

Flow from thy pen, slowly draining

Pours out in rivers till nothing's remaining

How could I continue to scrawl

When all the words are drained out?

No, one day I will have to stop

For reach the end, you'll have to drop

So really, there's no point to dwell

I wish I could tell you this ends well

Dear reader, I think I could tell you this ends well
For I'm starting to crawl out from my shell
You say, my ideas will wither and die
But no, I'm sure they will survive
Perhaps you say there will be a day
Where I will have nothing left to say
But that is what inspiration is for
To pull from your friends, to ask for more
And so, don't be trapped by writing's evil spell
For I think I could tell you this ends well

Dear Me

Dear me

This is a message to the girl I used to be

Now, see

I'm trapped in confusion, can't claw my way free

They say

Keep your head up and you'll be okay

But all day

Worries brush my happiness away

Wish I could

Go back to when things were good

Then I would

Stay in the time where life understood

How I feel

All the sorrows don't seem that real

But reveals

A core of feathers instead of steel

Still try

To look up and hope I don't cry

Can't deny

The tears still gather inside my eyes

Now I rely

On burying the truth under the lies

No reply

When I ask myself, who am I?

Hush, Child

Hush, child, look at me now
How much uncertainty do you think I'll allow?
You say you're not pretty, shamed by your face
But inside, you have love that looks can't erase
Look at your eyes, a warm, melting brown
They're too beautiful for you to look down

Hush, child, look at me now
Do you think you're subject to jeers from the crowd?
You say you're not strong, weak inside and out
But you crawl with a strength others run without
Inside you hold burdens, a pain that won't leave
You bear it with strength others don't perceive

Hush, child, look at me now

What manner of hate do you think I would vow?

You say that your world is surrounded by pain

But there's a light inside you that hasn't yet drained

People think you unlucky, ash without sparks

Don't forget, your light will shine bright in the dark

Hush, child, look at me now

Do you think I won't cheer after your final bow?

You say that you scorn, unkind in your flaws

But there's always a kindness that re-attracts applause

For our human selves can change, not set in stone

There's always joy left that we've never known

Hush, child, look at me now

No, don't plead with those furrowed brows

You've never needed help searching, and you never will

For your bucket of feelings is waiting to bc filled

So child, go now, go search for more joy

For hope is one thing self-doubt can't destroy

Drifting Piano Tales

incandescent notes tell stories
each press of a key, a touch of the loom
weaving out bright colors like a voice,
telling the tale of the world
the horrors of death in grieving minor
staccato beats for the drums of war
major for the arrival of peace
thousands of fingers weaving stories
a tapestry of music to trap the past
with more music to be made
looking towards the future
and all the hopes we have
glistening with each press
of a key.

A Childhood Fairytale

A valiant knight in shining armor
A beauteous princess seeking a hand
A kind and charming bounteous farmer
That becomes ruler of the mystic land

A cascade of bejeweled fairytales
Embedded in endless pages
Thousands of magical paths and trails
The stories of many ages

A velvety cushion beneath my feet
A fantasy in my mind
An image of a world complete

With whimsical humankind

Flipping through the ancient tomes
Imagining the scenes
A tale of petite garden gnomes
Of princes and kings and queens

Oh, how I miss being right at home
With my magical little friends
Even this dainty little poem
Can't capture how each tale ends

Sitting on the worn out couch
The book within my sight
Upon the plush seat I slouch
Joy and peace and delight

Gently placing the book in my hand
I feast on the creation of word

Little did I understand

These reveries would be deferred

Oh, how my life has unfurled

How change comes out of the blue

How I wish that our veridical world

Could be like a fairytale too

Picking Flowers

One, two, three, four
Pick one flower, then some more
Bouquets piled, one then two
Wither away on the floor

Cherry blossoms, falling down
Pink for love all around
Petals dropping from the sky
Breaking, like love, on the ground
Cherry blossoms, in the air
White for beauty that we share
Leave behind when we die
Blank canvases, clean and bare

Orchids, brilliance to enthrall

Purple, royalty in us all

Exclude the silent, ban the weak

Wipe the shame and stand tall

Orchids, flawless in every way

Like we strive to be every day

Nobody has a perfect streak

Like orchids, first to be plucked away

Lavenders, piercing towards the sky

Indigo, power to defy

Be the best, at the top

Thrones built on truths and lies

Lavenders, filling up the field

Violet, to dreams all will yield

We'll have everything, and then drop

Powers, together they'll wield

One, two, three, four

Many people fighting for more

Regrets piled, one then two

Like flowers in their regal war

Four, three, two, one

Can’t fit in? Turn and run

Pink, purple, violet, blue

Sadly, this war’s already won

We are just like flowers too

For another war has just begun

The Chapter Before

Things change, things are different, they shatter and then reform

Sometimes it feels, that you can't find, the calm inside the storm

This was me, so long ago, when I moved to a brand new realm

Sailing unknown seas, everyone gone, scared behind the helm

I arrived, in a place brand new, lonely and hidden away

Not knowing what exactly might come, following the next day

Standing alone, a girl walked up, and looked me in the eye

Then a miracle, finally occurred, as she smiled and said hi

From that day on, I realized that flowers, won't bloom under a clear sky

And that caterpillars, when they curl alone, become a butterfly

That none of us, like these words, will rest perfectly in a line

That our life can change, and so can I, for we don't have to rhyme

When things are reversed, and life is flipped, sometimes you remember

That through the ashes, of your past, you find a memory of an ember

Expand your heart, when you begin to feel, it hoping and aching for more

You can't start the next chapter of your life, if you keep re-reading the one before

The Sun Was A Burn

The sun was a burn.

And I only come out at night.

And that's what I think as I sit quietly in the meadow, blades of grass tickling my nose, a canopy of night laid wide above my head

Shooting stars sprint across the sky, like the fallen angels burning, burning, flying down and hitting the horizon in strings of magical thread

I only come out at night, because I still remember the way the sun caught in your hair, bright yellow rays creating sparks in your diamond eyes

I think of the light of day catching on your white teeth as you smiled, and I have flashbacks of you running towards the sunrise

Under the cover of night, my sack of burdens is hidden, concealed by the dark, and no one else needs to see and remind me of the better days

The memory of the sun was a burn, and still is, because you left a trace of yourself in my broken heart that will never fully go away

And I only come out at night, because

The sun was a burn.

PART 3
FANTASY & THOUGHTS

Freedom of Forever

Meet me at midnight, under the sky, in the forest of my dreams

We'll count the stars within our souls and dance to moonlight's beams

Travel to the lands, where the birds sing, in the distance of the world

Where the sun goes down in the evening light with the love of swirls and whirls

The place where the clouds, and the fish in the water, float in a sea of bliss

And together we paint the light of dawn, coloring our reminisce

The place where the stars never set and we smile with

whomever

Frolic to realms, to joy and hope in the freedom of forever

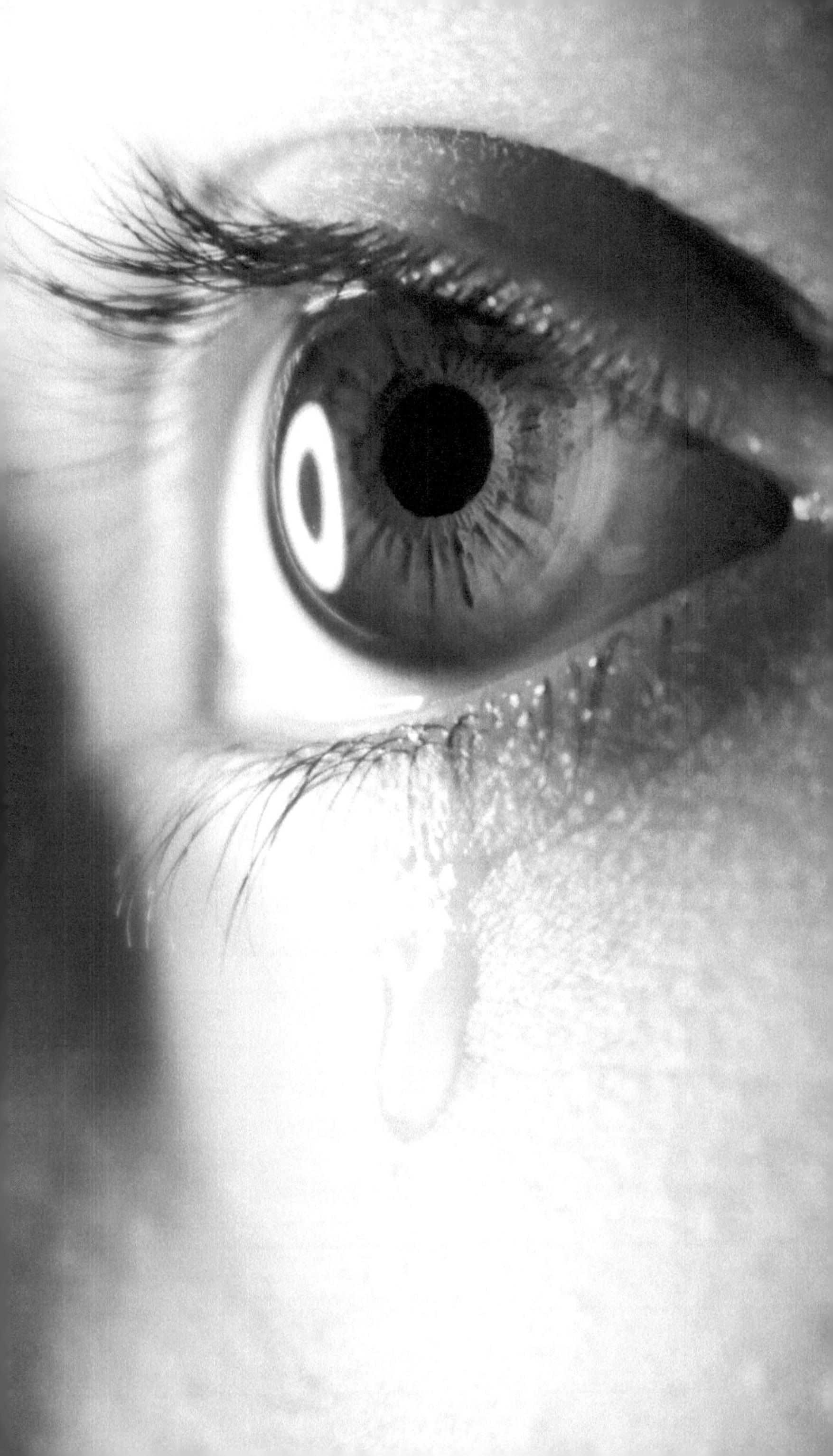

In the Time of a Falling Tear

She could still remember that day
When the world came crashing down
The throne shattered, collapsing glass
And she forever lost her crown

Inside, she was in despair
The glass sharp, making her bleed
But she let the blood flow, let it drip
Why be sad? He has been freed

To all, she may have looked the same
But it was only a mirage, foolish hope
Dangling from the edge of a cliff

She lost her hold on the rope

It only took a few, short seconds
For him to say his last goodbye
She only shed a single tear, just one
But a thousand poured inside

She made sure her face stayed composed
Her eyes understanding and clear
But her heart shriveled up and died
In the time of that falling tear

She still remembered that breaking day
But now, without breaking
For her heart has been patched back up
No one else's for the taking

He's kind, and he'll stay forever
Remain, always, by her side

Instead of taking the throne, he'll share
Bestow the crown to her with pride

There might be just one part of her
That time will never heal
But her joy, when compared to the pain
Is infinite times more real

That first time, when he said goodbye
She thought her world was ending
But that was only the start
Of a story just beginning

And now, today, him and her become one
Stay together for a thousand more years
So much joy as they said "I do"
In the time of many falling tears

A Safe Haven

The forest is dark, leering shadows waiting, malicious yellow eyes

Strange animals chitter, spiders crawling, piercing ominous cries

But still, I keep walking

The forest trail is barely visible through the thick tangle of weeds

Who knows what monstrosities these shadows will breed

But still, I keep walking

The inky black night sky is hidden by the dense canopy of leaves

The moon's light barely pierces through the dim forest eaves

But still, I keep walking

Because through the darkness, something calls to me

Something lurking deep inside me, that I will finally see

So I keep walking

I know, just some innate sense, that the forest will break somewhere

A clearing, open to the moonlight, I just know it is there

So I keep walking

The clearing, I can see it, so luminous, before the dark picks up again

On the other side, is shadows, but I can see the bright forest den

So I keep walking

I reach the clearing, moonlight washing over me, dizzy with sensation

This place, this is who I am, my very existence, my creation

So I stop walking

But something is still calling to me, something not in this safe haven

Something that lurks inside the darkness, shadows unshaven

So I stop walking

But it still pulls, and something inside me wishes to go in and embrace the gloom

I can't resist, and I walk in warily, only to find… my impending doom

I have walked into the dead man's tomb

The swirling dead, so many people that have been lured, have been attracted here

To feed the dead soul of this darkened forest. How foolish I am, how real my fear

The walking once more begins…

It Was Just a Dream

I remember it all, every moment
All the laughter, all the tears
It doesn't seem real, that small component
Us drifting away over the years

It seems surreal, the people I lost
So many later, so many before
I never seem to remember the cost
When I let my heart make room for more

All the broken, left behind connections
The lost advisors and friends
But we all go in different directions
And our path together ends

It seems strange, when I think back
To the memories that we share
When the rooms clear and the bags pack
And it's like they were never there

But now I think of those friends long gone
Maybe everything that happened was right
That before the sun rises at dawn
There has to have been a night

That the reason they were left behind
And never come back later
And our hearts remain undefined
To be filled with something greater

But even as I continue to grow
There's times I must redeem
The fact that those times so long ago
Seem like they were just a dream

My Fault This Time

I still remember

The way you smiled

Light up the world

For miles and miles

Brighten the nights

With a million stars

And now we are

Miles and years apart

You used to shine

The sun, during the day

But now your light

Has faded away

I still remember
The way you spoke
Like crackling flames
Clear of smoke
Each word with meaning
Every sentence strong
You don't know how
It was to me all along
Every calming phrase
That passed through my ears
I replay it, now and forever
Though it hurts to hear

I still remember
How you loved nature
From warm, summer sun
To ice cold glaciers
You would sit in the garden
For hours upon hours

Only I would know

You were friends with the flowers

Strung every plant

Together like beads

And every flower you planted

Bore another seed

I still remember

How your face had broken

When you came up to me

And final words were spoken

All that pain on your face

That sorrow and grief

A fake pain, perhaps

I no longer believe

And I know there's no meaning

In these silly rhymes

But I just want you to know

It's my fault this time

Trickster, Trickster

trickster, trickster, ready when you are
the rainbow's end lies not very far
when the treasure lies at my feet
you can't open my shield, nor touch my scars

trickster, trickster, you think you're best
of fraud and words is your side of the test
but wait, just wait, i'm almost there
soon i'll take your place in the home of red

trickster, trickster, you believe that you've won
but our war is beginning, far from being done
my shadow will fall, like the darkness at dusk

did you think you could outrun the setting sun?

trickster, trickster, look towards the dawn
see blood red clouds the sun shines upon?
my throne will be built upon land of blood
careful now, I’ll be there when you’re gone

If I Could Fly...

If I could fly
I'd travel to the stars
Touch those diamonds of the sky
The lights that we were granted
To light up our darkness
The smiles
That guide our way
Through the blackness of the night
The compass
That directs our wild journeys

If I could fly
I'd touch the sun

Join the birds in the sky

Listen to the bright birdsong

Gasp at the brightness that meets my eyes

See the light that wakes us at morn

That banishes the darkness

But makes the stars relinquish

To a new dawn

Feel the warmth that guides us

That has been our greatest ally

If I could fly

I'd see the world

Blow with the wind

Let it show me the wonders

On our Earth

None has seen

I'd flow with the rivers

Let it take me down mountains

Over the falls

Across the tundra

And out into the ocean

If I could fly

I'd fly past the people

Those bright souls

That inhabit our world

See that kindness

See people feel joy and love

See people feel pain and sorrow

But then overcome it

Overcome the difficulties

Overcome the challenges

And smile again at the stars in the sky

If I could fly...

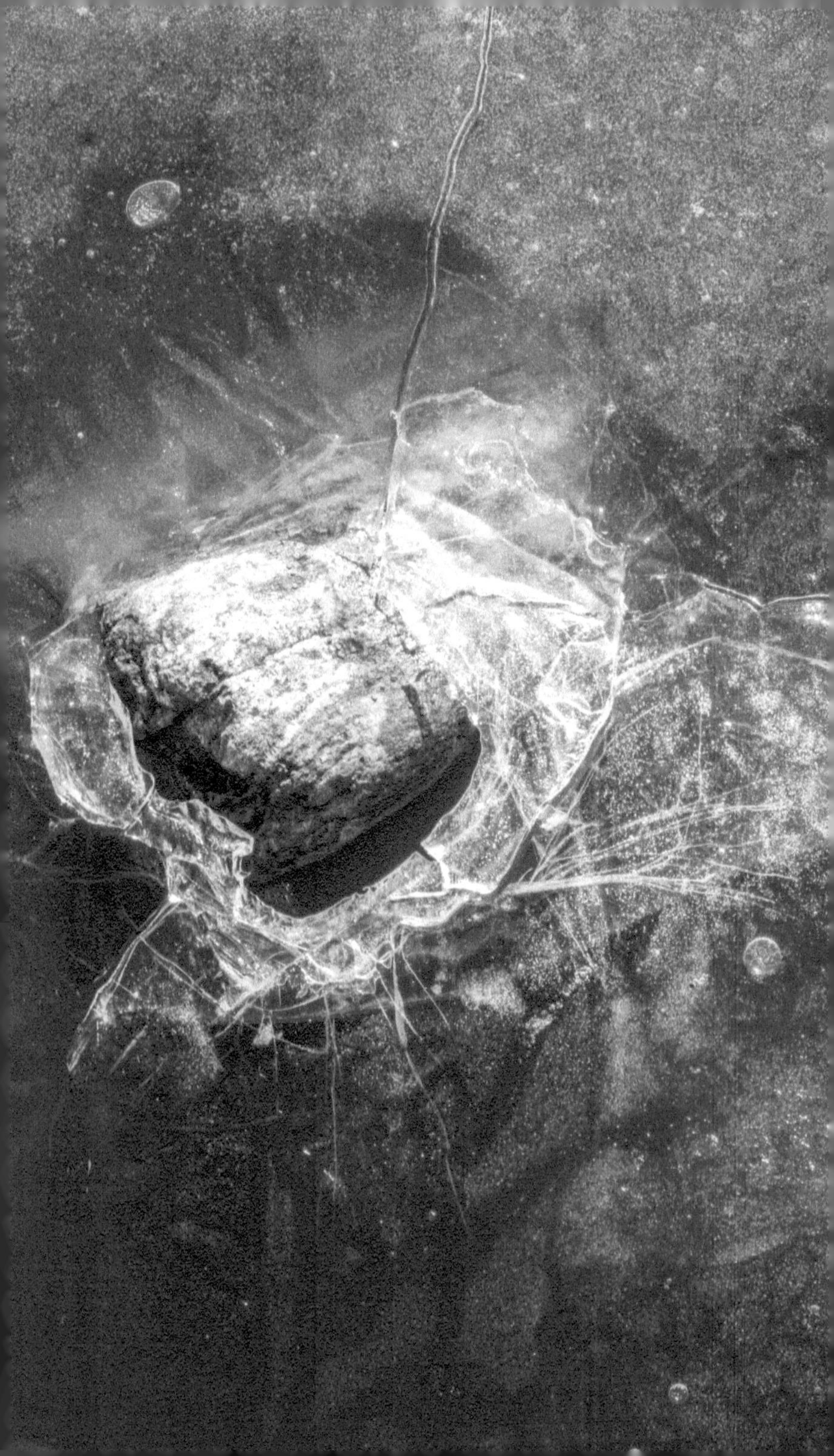

A Million Fractures

I'll put my life inside a prism
Fit myself into glass molds
Let it fracture to a million colors
Of black and white and gold

I'll fit my soul inside the rainbow
That spills out from its sides
The million colors that swirl and prod
Inside our curious eyes

I'll shove my heart inside a prism
Beat down the feelings till they're dead
Or else they will overwhelm and kill

The joy in me instead

I'll light my being inside the rainbow
Let it shatter, let it break
Perhaps if I were floating in shards
There'll be no room for all the hate

I'll drift my ghost inside a prism
No light in the transparent form
A million clouds fill inside me
To block and weather the storm

I'll put my life inside a prism
Let diamonds shatter through my heart
With fractured light, I'll glue together
The glass still broken apart

Blood Won't Spill

trail leading deep into the forest of fools
moon's reflection, path into land beneath the pool
tirade of anger for trespassing the home
the innocent walks moonlight's path alone
those of the land guard with viscous scars
but of the sea wish to connect the breaking heart
one land for peace, and the other for war
naive youth spawns hate like never before
kingdom of land hopes water burns alive
forgetting that the water is what makes land thrive

at the end, when 12 moon cycles come to a close
to a gathering that kingdom's rulers know

one time of peace, no bloodshed nor war

to sign the agreement that's saved them before

because the land holds blood, long time foes

apart by forbidden path the river flows

and so at this end, they gather here

to hope blood won't spill for another year

Thoughts of Writing

Churning thoughts
They swirl and prod
In my mind
Turning and turning
Seeking escape,
But no sound comes
No way to speak
The vast waters roiling
Inside of me
Waves tossing, creatures
Of great depths
Waiting and waiting
So I pour then onto paper

Let the ocean

Guide the pen

And the wind blow

The sails on the boat

The thoughts

Spill out in ink

The shapes and words

Swirling and swirling

Maybe I can't

Speak them

Like others can go on

Talking and talking

But I can keep

Writing and writing

www.ingramcontent.com/pod-product-compliance
Ingram Content Group UK Ltd.
Pitfield, Milton Keynes, MK11 3LW, UK
UKHW040556210726
13854UKWH00007B/60